My
Kindergarten
Workbook

This book belongs to:

Way to Go!

After completing each activity, color a star to track how much you've done!

1 2 3 4
5 6 7 8 9 10
11 12 13 14 15 16
17 18 19 20 21 22
23 24 25 26 27 28

29	30	31	32	33	34
35	36	37	38	39	40
41	42	43	44	45	46
47	48	49	50	51	52
53	54	55	56	57	58
59	60	61	62	63	64
65	66	67	68	69	70

My Kindergarten Workbook

101
Games and Activities
to Support Kindergarten Skills

BRITTANY LYNCH

Illustrations by Robin Boyer

ROCKRIDGE
PRESS

Contents

Note to Parents

Dear Parents,

Kindergarten is a big step in a child's life. Kindergarteners are making new friends and navigating a new classroom environment, all while absorbing new concepts such as literacy, math, science, and social studies.

My Kindergarten Workbook was designed to reinforce many of the skills your child is about to discover. Use it to give your child a boost before entering the classroom, to offer extra support at home while kindergarten is in session, or even as a fun review over the summer so that newly-learned skills stay fresh.

As a former kindergarten teacher with a master's degree in early childhood education, I know what children need to be successful learners, and I know that children learn best when they are engaged in what they are doing. The 101 games and activities in this workbook were designed to keep kids entertained and motivated. Through coloring, mazes, search-and-find puzzles, and other fun games, your child will practice essential kindergarten skills such as letters and reading, numbers, sequencing, early math facts, and more—and they won't even realize that they are learning!

The subjects are color-coded by section to make finding the material easy. Within each section, the activities start off simple and slowly increase in difficulty. Completing the easiest ones first will allow your child's confidence to build, and your little one will quickly become curious and eager to see what comes next!

Children learn at different speeds, so it's okay if your child needs a little support when working through the book. Read the directions to them and help them get started, if needed. If an activity seems to frustrate your child, feel free to skip a page and try again at another time. The goal of *My Kindergarten Workbook* is to support your child's kindergarten skills and to make learning fun.

So, let's have some fun!

Brittany Lynch

I. Alphabet Warm-Up

Point to each letter and say its name. Then say the beginning sound for the picture that starts with that letter.

2. Amazing A

Trace the uppercase and lowercase letters.

A a

A is for apple.

A A A A A A

a a a a a

What is hidden in the picture below? Color every **A** and **a** to find out!

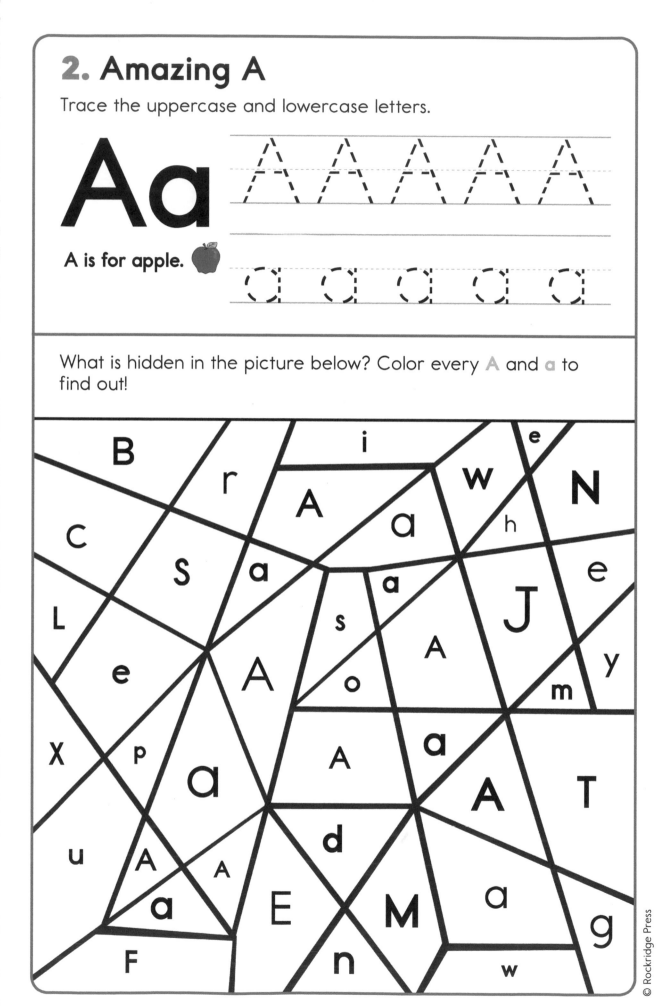

My Kindergarten Workbook

© Rockridge Press

3. Beautiful B

Trace the uppercase and lowercase letters.

Bb

B is for ball.

B B B B B

b b b b b

Circle 4 things in the basket that begin with the letter B.

4. Cuddly C

Trace the uppercase and lowercase letters.

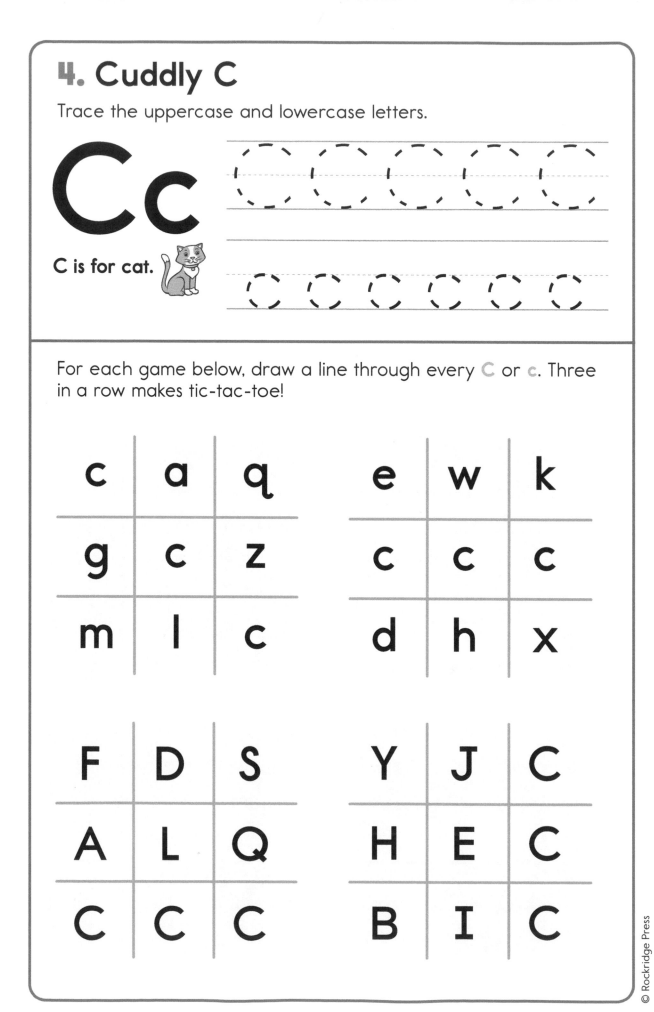

C is for cat.

For each game below, draw a line through every C or c. Three in a row makes tic-tac-toe!

c	a	q
g	c	z
m	l	c

e	w	k
c	c	c
d	h	x

F	D	S
A	L	Q
C	C	C

Y	J	C
H	E	C
B	I	C

My Kindergarten Workbook

5. Daring D

Trace the uppercase and lowercase letters.

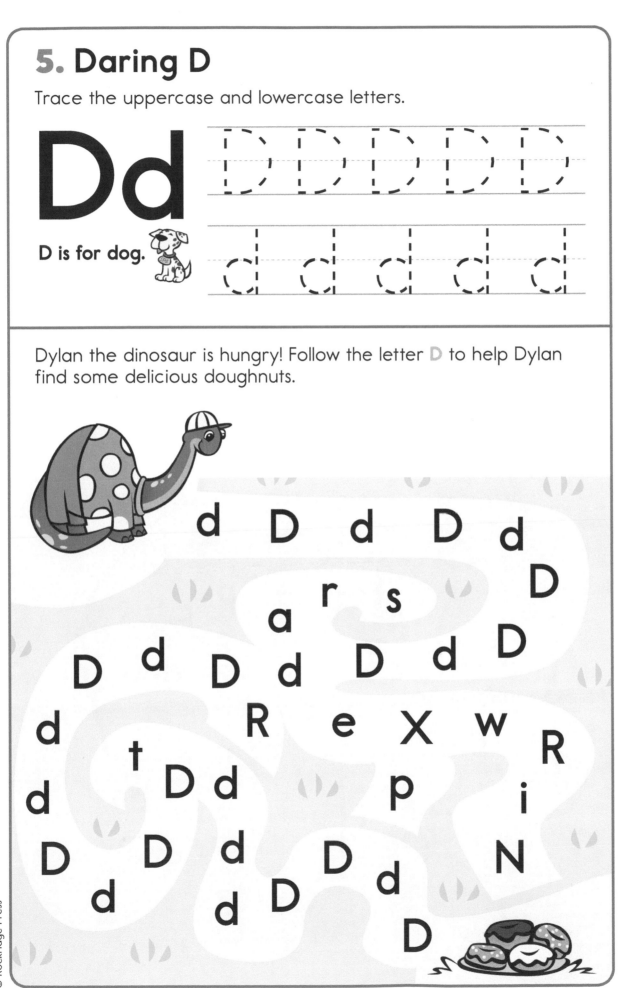

D is for dog.

Dylan the dinosaur is hungry! Follow the letter D to help Dylan find some delicious doughnuts.

6. Energetic E

Trace the uppercase and lowercase letters.

E e

E is for egg.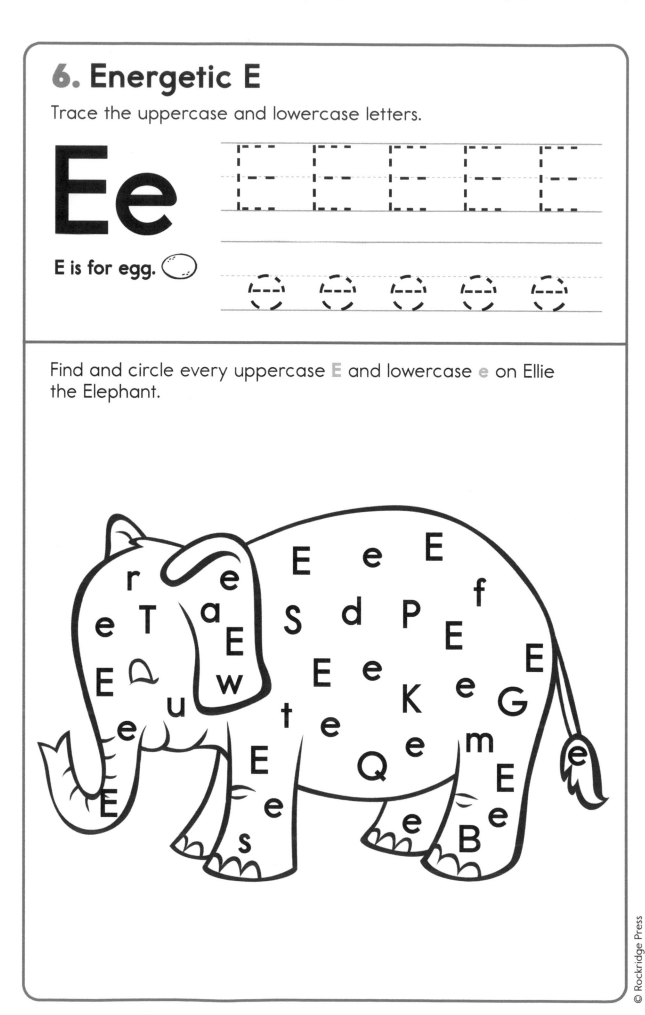

Find and circle every uppercase **E** and lowercase **e** on Ellie the Elephant.

My Kindergarten Workbook

7. Fantastic F

Trace the uppercase and lowercase letters.

F f

F is for fish.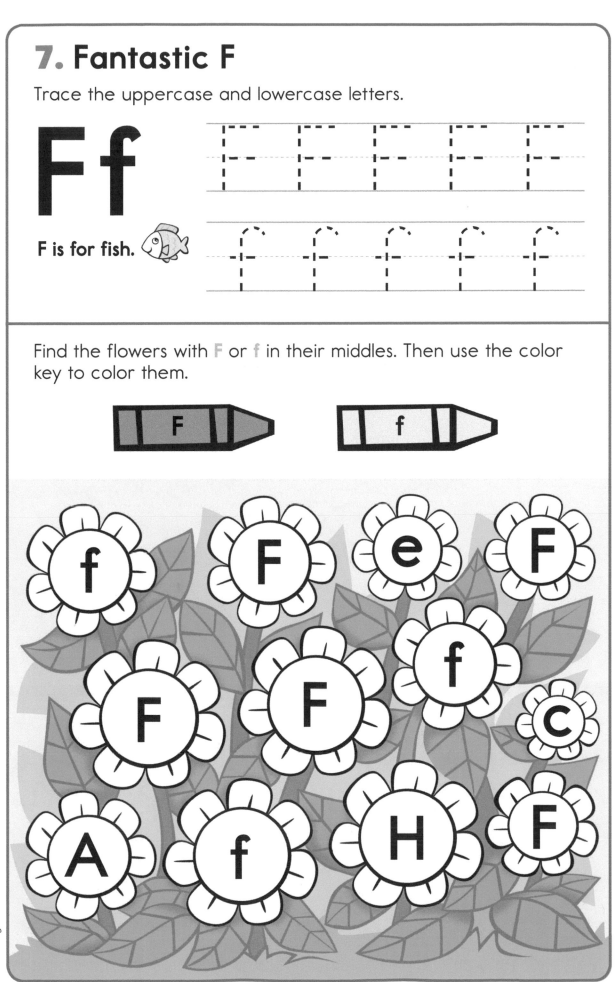

Find the flowers with **F** or **f** in their middles. Then use the color key to color them.

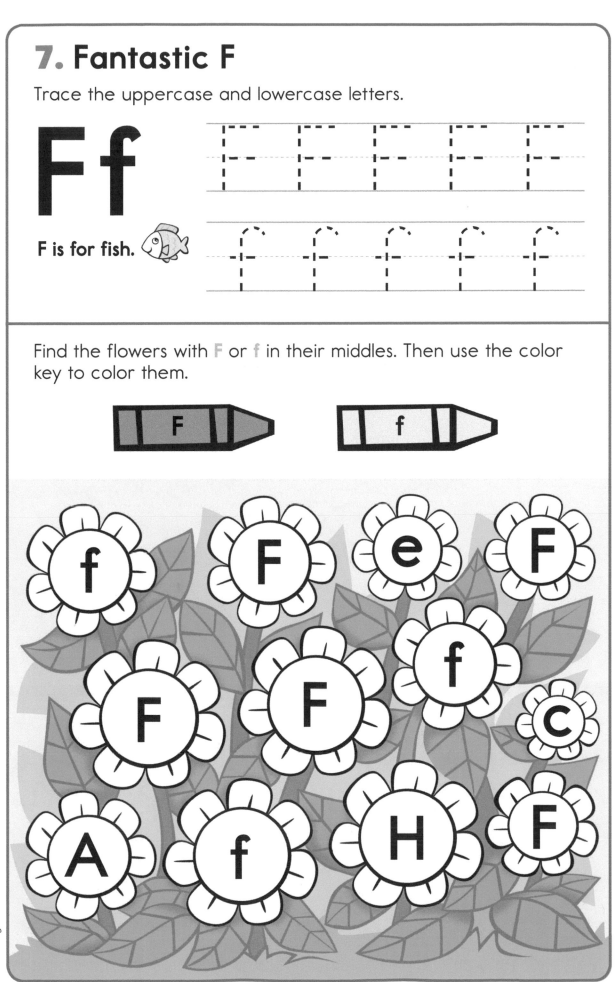

© Rockridge Press

8. Great G

Trace the uppercase and lowercase letters.

Gg

G is for goose.

Find and circle all the hidden objects that begin with the letter G.

Word Bank

grapes gorilla girl glove gate

9. Match-It-Up Letter Review

Draw a line from each uppercase letter to its matching lowercase letter.

10. Happy H

Trace the uppercase and lowercase letters.

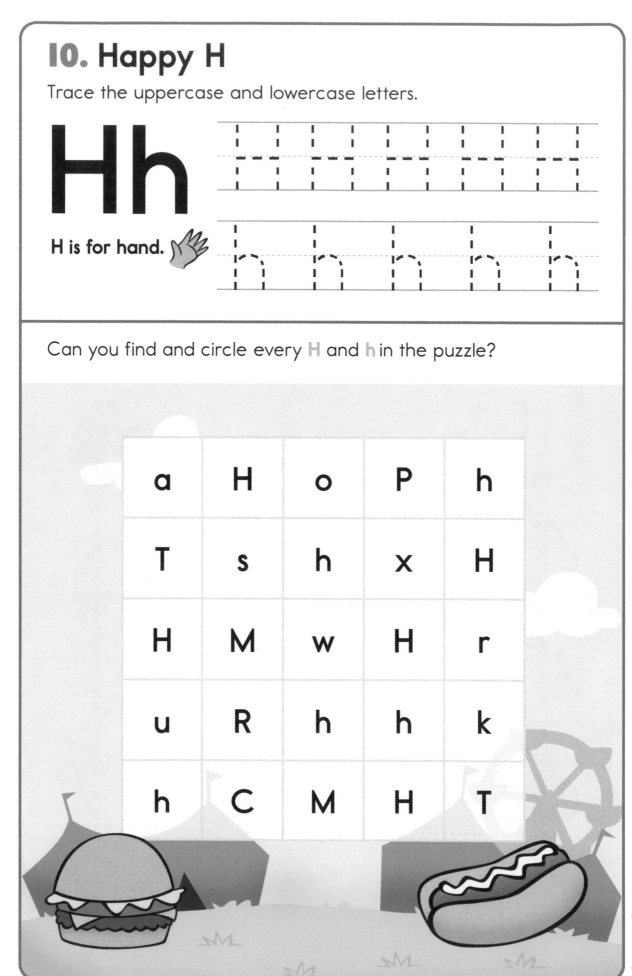

H is for hand.

Can you find and circle every H and h in the puzzle?

a	H	o	P	h
T	s	h	x	H
H	M	w	H	r
u	R	h	h	k
h	C	M	H	T

11. Intelligent I

Trace the uppercase and lowercase letters.

I i

I is for iguana.

Color each space with an **I brown** and each space with an **i pink** to see a yummy picture!

12. Jiggly J

Trace the uppercase and lowercase letters.

Jj

J is for jacket.

J J J J J J

j j j j j j

Put a ✔ on each jellybean with a **J** or a **j**.

My Kindergarten Workbook

13. Kind K

Trace the uppercase and lowercase letters.

Kk

K is for kite.

K K K K K

k k k k k

For the game below, draw a line through the things that start with the letter K. Three in a row makes tic-tac-toe!

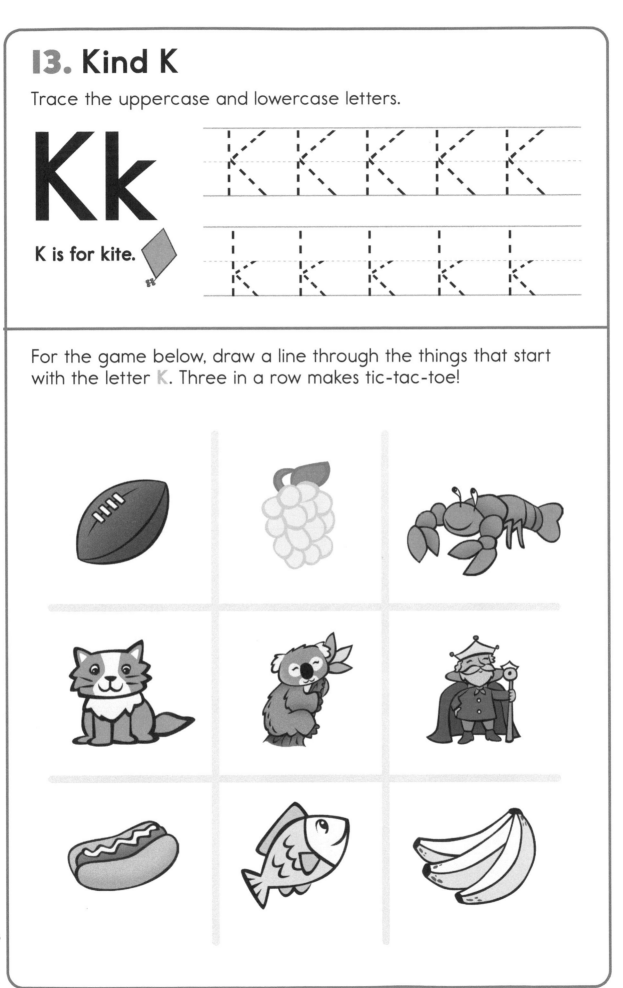

14. Lovely L

Trace the uppercase and lowercase letters.

L l

L is for leaf.

Oh no! Lizzie the lizard has dropped her lemon lollipop. Follow the letter Ls to help Lizzie find it.

My Kindergarten Workbook

15. Mighty M

Trace the uppercase and lowercase letters.

Mm

M is for moon.

M M M M M

m m m m m m

Find and circle **5** things in the kitchen that begin with the letter **M**.

16. Nice N

Trace the uppercase and lowercase letters.

Nn

N is for nest.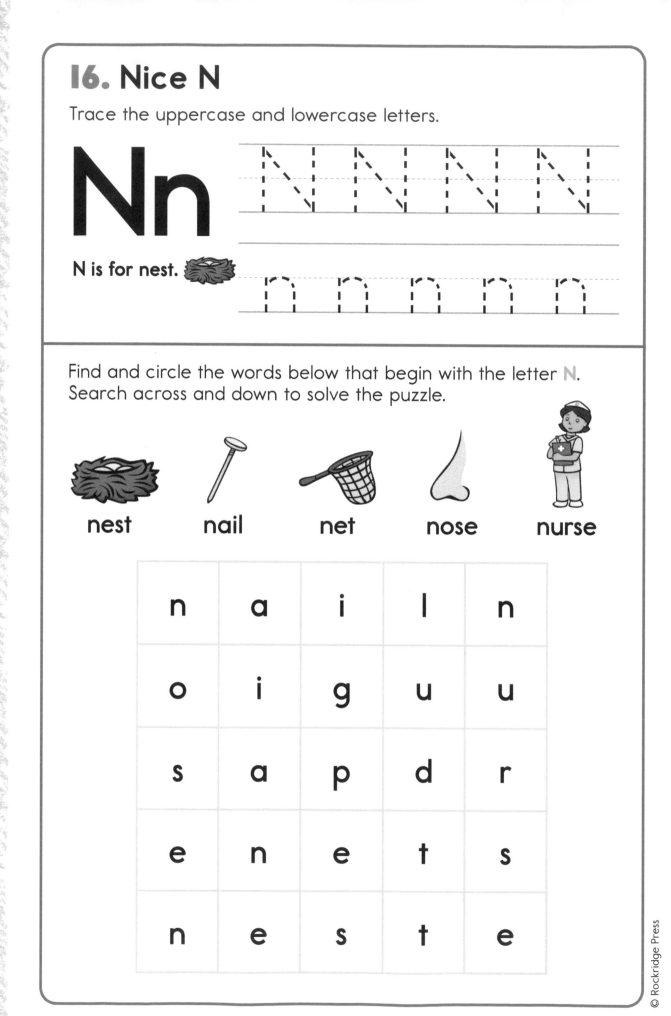

N N N N N

n n n n n

Find and circle the words below that begin with the letter N. Search across and down to solve the puzzle.

nest   nail   net   nose   nurse

n	a	i	l	n
o	i	g	u	u
s	a	p	d	r
e	n	e	t	s
n	e	s	t	e

17. Dot-to-Dot Letter Review

Start at the red stars. Connect the dots from **h** to **n**. Then connect the dots from **H** to **N**, and see two flying friends.

18. Outstanding O

Trace the uppercase and lowercase letters.

O o

O is for olive.

Find and circle the hidden pictures that begin with the letter O.

Word Bank

ox ostrich
olive owl

19. Peppy P

Trace the uppercase and lowercase letters.

P p

P is for penguin.

P P P P P

p p p p p

Use the word bank and the picture clues to complete the crossword puzzle.

Word Bank

pig pumpkin pencil
puzzle plum pizza

20. Quiet Q

Trace the uppercase and lowercase letters.

Qq

Q is for queen.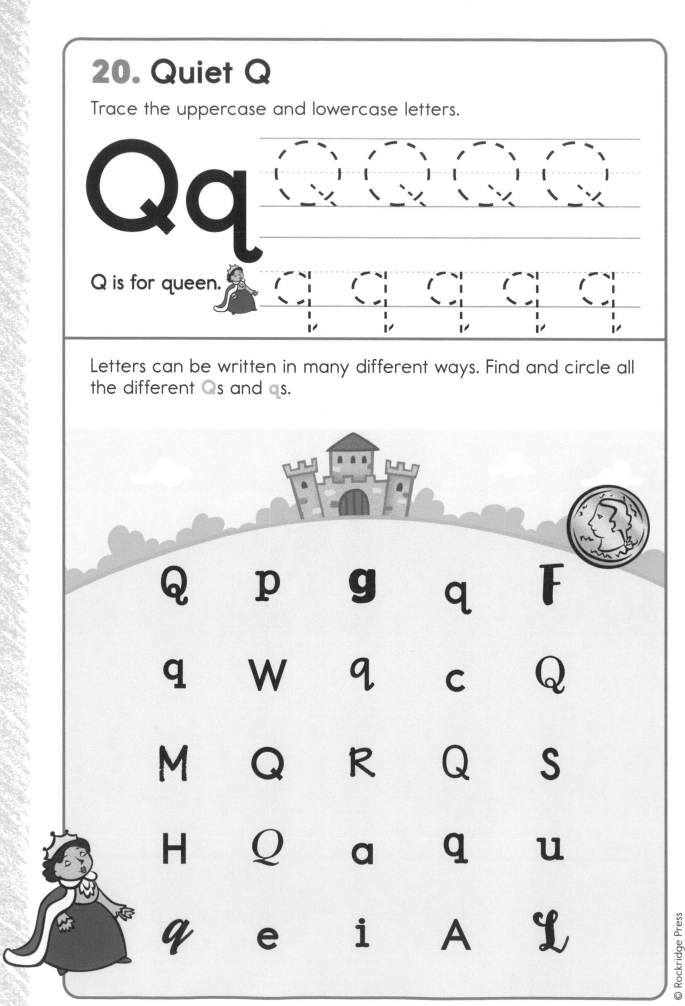

Letters can be written in many different ways. Find and circle all the different Qs and qs.

Q   p   g   q   F

q   w   q   c   Q

M   Q   R   Q   S

H   Q   a   q   u

q   e   i   A   L

My Kindergarten Workbook

21. Relaxed R

Trace the uppercase and lowercase letters.

Rr

R is for robot.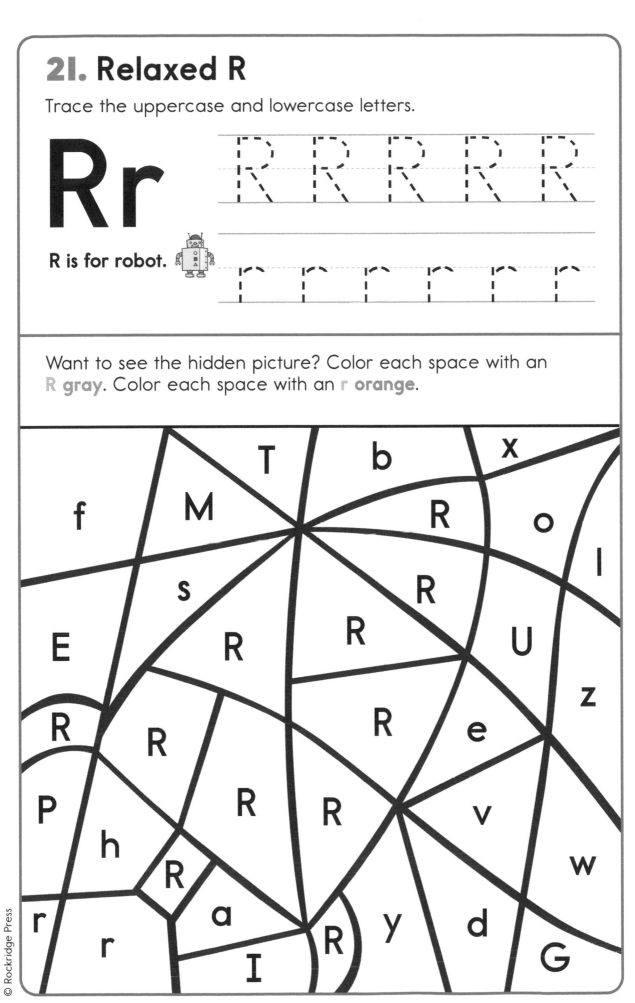

R R R R R

r r r r r r

Want to see the hidden picture? Color each space with an
R gray. Color each space with an r orange.

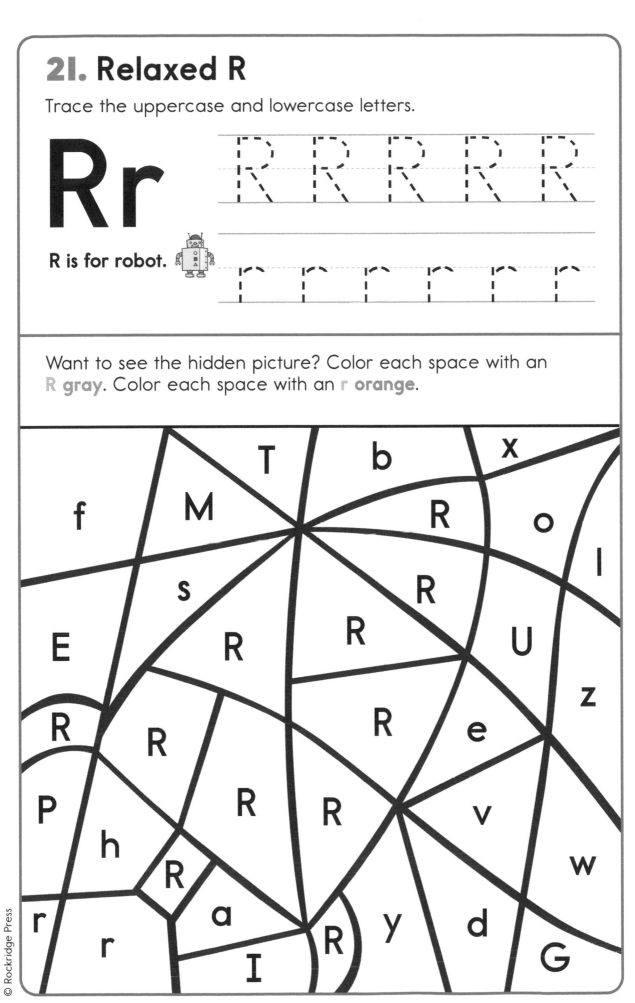

22. Super S

Trace the uppercase and lowercase letters.

Ss

S is for sock.

S S S S S

s s s s s

Find and circle 4 things in the picture that begin with the letter S.

23. Terrific T

Trace the uppercase and lowercase letters.

T t

T is for tiger.

Start at the red star. Connect the dots with the letter T to finish the picture.

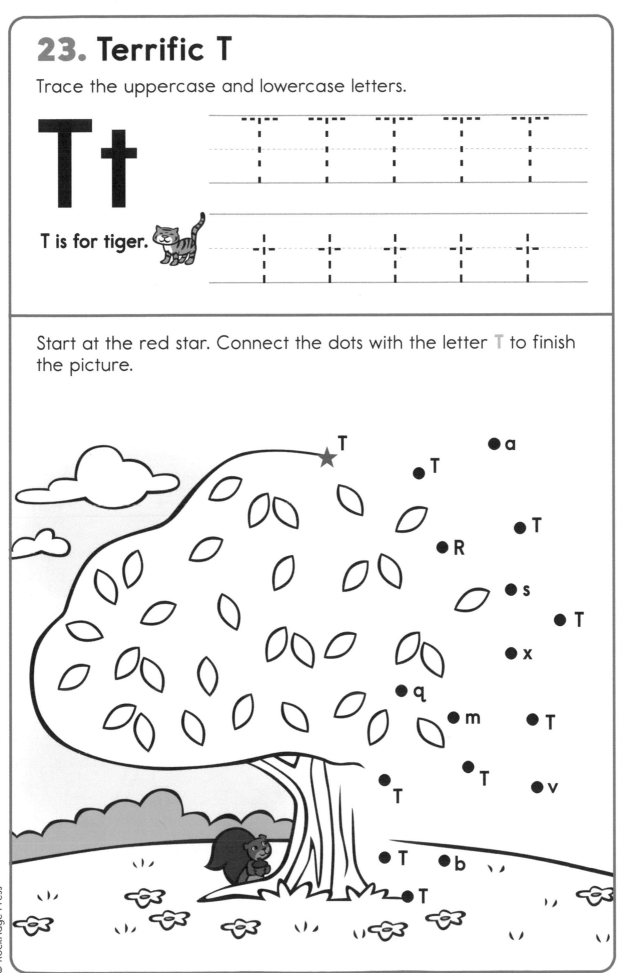

24. Color It! Letter Review

Use the color key to color this *moo*-ving scene.

25. Useful U

Trace the uppercase and lowercase letters.

Uu

U is for up.

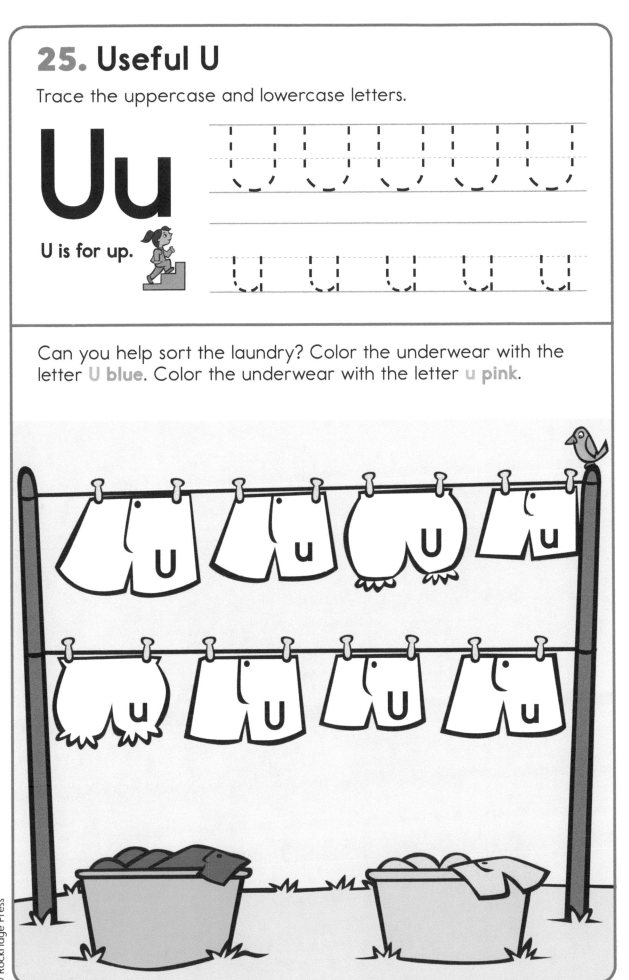

Can you help sort the laundry? Color the underwear with the letter U **blue**. Color the underwear with the letter u **pink**.

26. Violet V

Trace the uppercase and lowercase letters.

V v

V is for vest.

\/ \/ \/ \/ \/

v v v v v

In each game below, draw a line through the pictures that start with V. Three in a row makes tic-tac-toe!

My Kindergarten Workbook

27. Warm W

Trace the uppercase and lowercase letters.

W is for wagon.

Color each space with a **W** or **w blue** to see a hidden picture.

28. Excellent X

Trace the uppercase and lowercase letters.

Xx

X is for x-ray.

X X X X X

X X X X X

Follow the pictures that **end** with the letter **X** to help Pirate Max find his treasure.

29. Yummy Y

Trace the uppercase and lowercase letters.

Y y

Y is for yak.

Y Y Y Y Y

y y y y y

Find **5** pictures that begin with the letter Y and color them yellow.

| yam | yogurt | yo-yo | yak | yarn |

30. Zippy Z

Trace the uppercase and lowercase letters.

Zz

Z is for zipper.

Z Z Z Z Z

Z Z Z Z Z

Find and circle the words below that begin with the letter Z. Look across, down, and diagonally to solve the puzzle.

zoo   zebra   zipper   zero   zucchini

z	i	p	p	e	r	i	n
f	u	x	z	e	b	r	a
g	v	c	a	y	o	n	t
z	o	o	c	s	w	b	f
e	z	b	a	h	o	j	y
u	e	s	u	n	i	a	r
g	r	m	r	d	s	n	w
j	o	i	d	t	y	g	i

31. Match-It-Up Letter Review

Draw a line from each picture to its beginning sound.

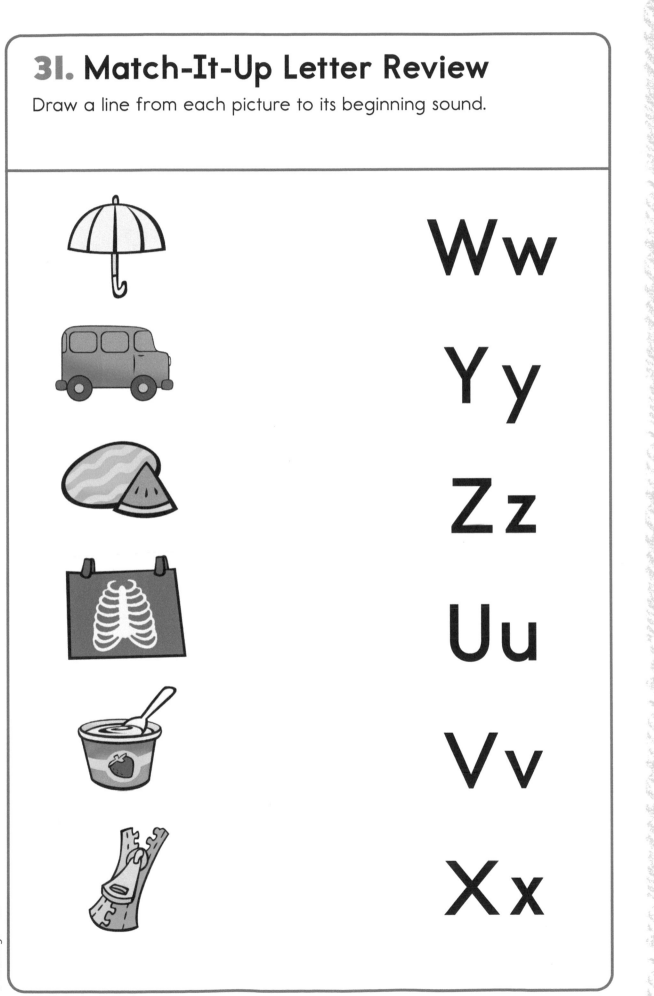

W w

Y y

Z z

U u

V v

X x

32. Monkey Maze

Get the monkey to the bananas by following the letters from **A** to **Z**.

My Kindergarten Workbook

33. Match the Rhyme

Draw a line to connect the words that rhyme.

34. Rhyme Time

Circle the **2** pictures in each row that rhyme. Put an **X** on the picture that does not rhyme.

bat   cat   mop

frog   milk   log

shark   bee   tree

swing   dress   ring

mug   rug   taco

35. Syllables Search

Say the name of the picture out loud. Then color in 1, 2, 3, or 4 circles for the number of syllables you hear.

36. Missing Middles

Cut out the vowels at the bottom and glue them in the correct spot to complete the word.

m		g

c		p

p		t

h		n

l		p

a e i o u

37. Bubblegum Vowels

Say the name of the picture in each gumball. Do you hear a short or long vowel sound in the word? Color each gumball according to the color code.

short vowel   long vowel

38. Consonant, Vowel, Consonant

Find and circle the CVC words below. Search across, down, and diagonally to solve the puzzle.

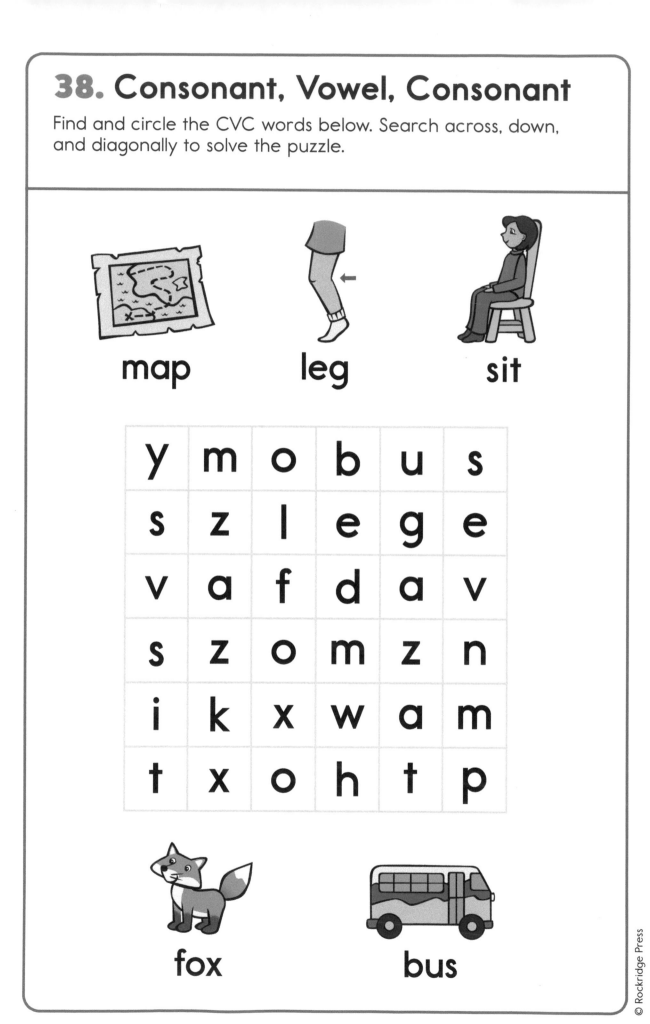

map   leg   sit

y	m	o	b	u	s
s	z	l	e	g	e
v	a	f	d	a	v
s	z	o	m	z	n
i	k	x	w	a	m
t	x	o	h	t	p

fox   bus

39. Sight Word Hunt

How many times can you find each sight word? Write the number in the box next to each word.

□ □ □ □ □ □
I   see   the   we   can   for

for   we   can   see

can   I   the   I

see   I   the   for

I   we   can   we

the   for   see   we   I   see

the   we   I

can   I   we

I   for   can   I

we   for

can   see

40. Can You Crossword?

Solve the clues and complete the crossword puzzle. Use the word bank to help you.

Across ➡

1. I _____ a brown dog.

3. Do you _____ my new hair?

4. I love _____ read!

Down ⬇

2. We _____ both 5.

5. _____ are my friend.

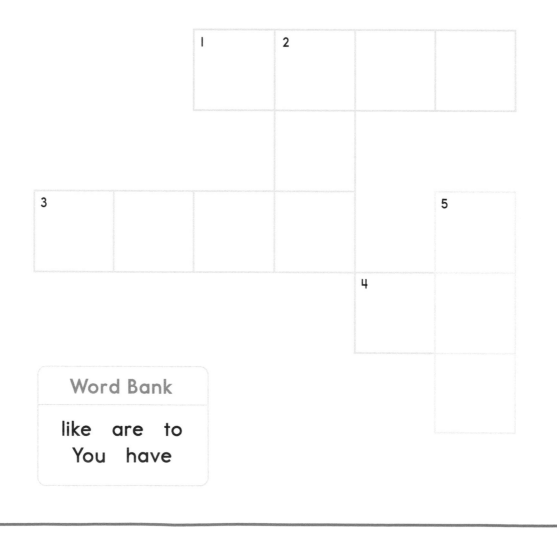

Word Bank

like   are   to
You   have

41. Sighting Sight Words

In each game below, draw a line through the sight word that appears 3 times. Three in a row makes tic-tac-toe!

play	my	is
with	is	with
is	said	here

with	said	here
my	play	here
is	is	here

with	play	my
said	play	here
my	play	said

here	play	said
with	with	with
is	said	my

with	here	play
play	said	is
my	my	my

said	here	is
play	said	with
play	my	said

42. Color by Sight Word

Use the color key to color the objects. Then color the rest of the picture.

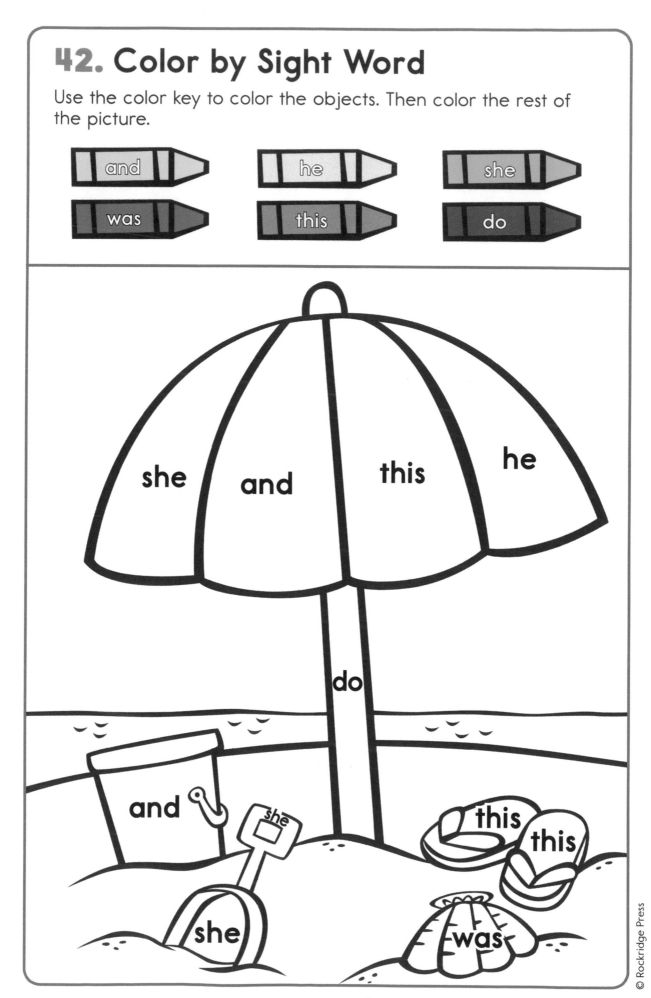

My Kindergarten Workbook

© Rockridge Press

43. Fishy Friends

Circle the pictures of the fish that are exactly the same. Then put an ✗ on all the rest.

Grouping Skills

53

44. Big or Small?

Color the spaces with **big** objects **yellow**. Color the spaces with **small** objects **blue**. Then find out what helps a garden grow!

45. Sorting Snacks

Decide if each snack at the bottom of the page is tall or short. Then, draw a line between each treat and the plate it should be on.

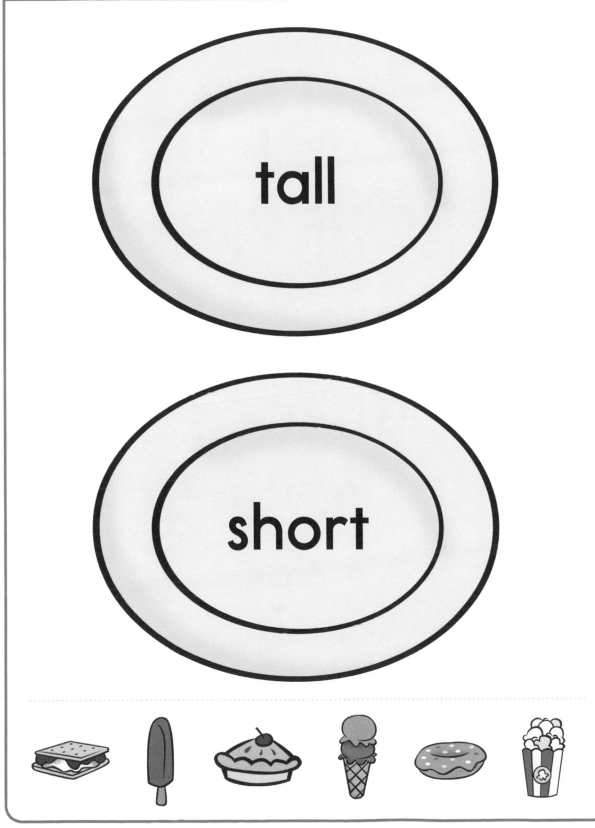

46. Strong Sam

Help Sam get stronger by following the path that has heavy objects for him to lift.

My Kindergarten Workbook

© Rockridge Press

47. Above or Below?

Color the pictures that are above the table **purple**. Color the pictures that are below the table **orange**.

48. Where is the Bear?

Put a ✔ where the bear is in front of an object. Put an ✗ where the bear is behind an object.

49. Pond Life

Circle the animals **in** the pond. Put a box around the animals **out** of the pond.

50. Birthday Celebration

It's shaping up to be a great birthday! Use the color key to color all the shapes you find in the picture.

My Kindergarten Workbook

51. Swimming in the Sea

Use the color key to color the picture so these friends can swim together.

© Rockridge Press

52. Clowning Around

Follow this pattern to help the clown find his funny friends.

53. Painting a Pattern

Circle which paintbrush comes next in each pattern.

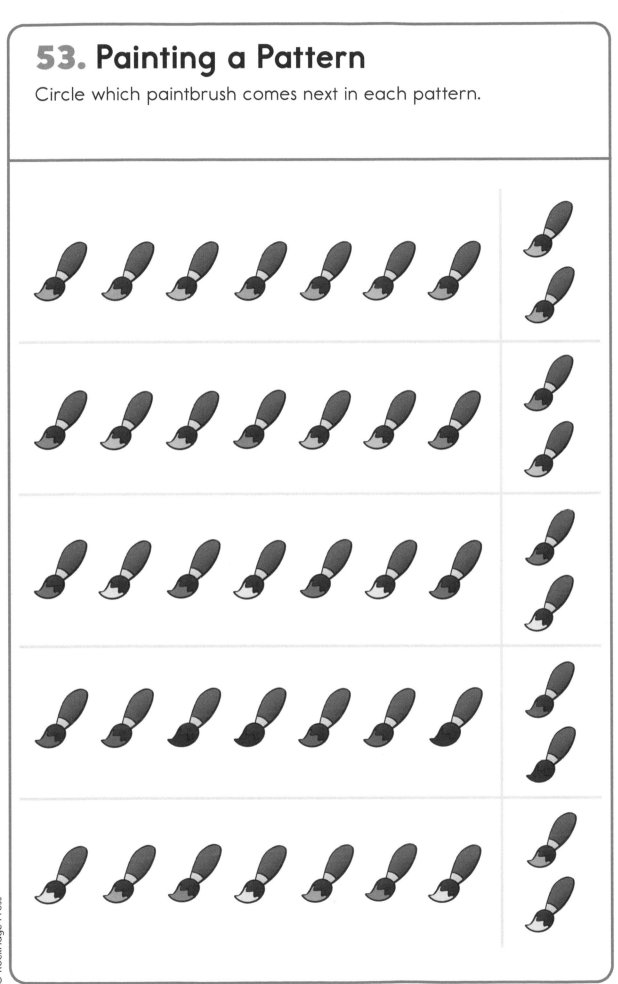

54. Crayon Colors

Color the missing crayon to complete each pattern.

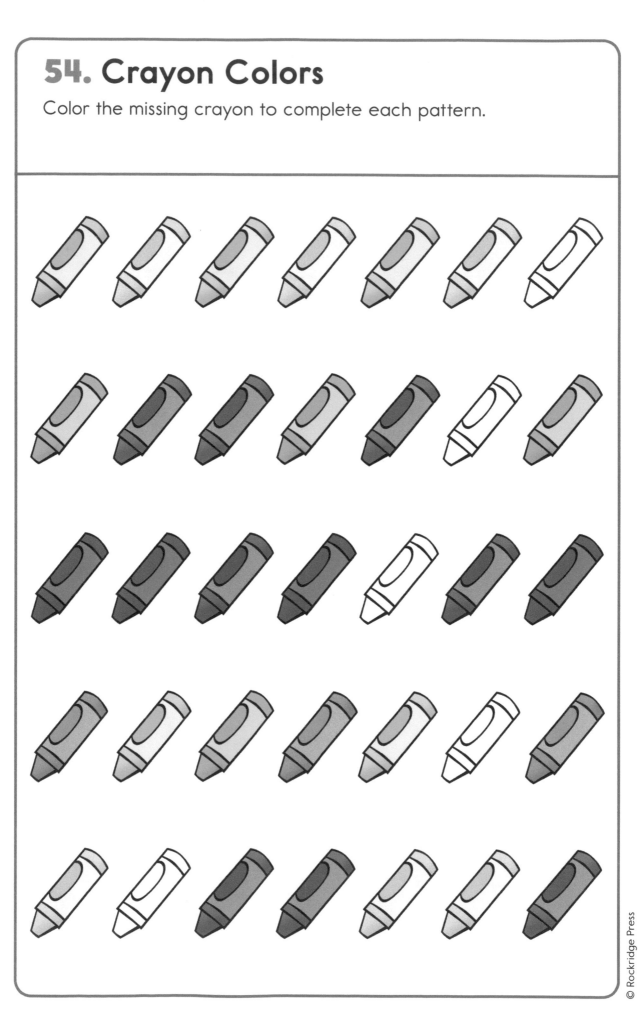

My Kindergarten Workbook

© Rockridge Press

55. All Aboard the Number Train!

Trace the numbers 1 to 20 and say each one out loud.

56. Counting Candles

Count the candles on each birthday cake. Color the circle with the correct number.

My Kindergarten Workbook

57. Connect Four

See the number in the flower? Can you find that number repeated 4 times in a row? Draw a line to connect them. Search across or down to solve the puzzle.

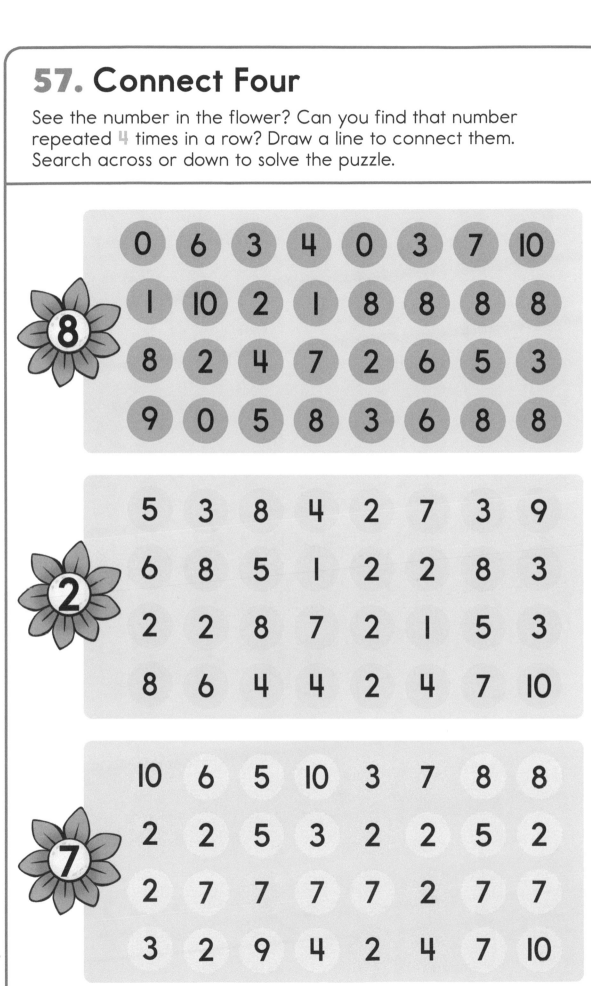

Flower: 8

0	6	3	4	0	3	7	10
1	10	2	1	8	8	8	8
8	2	4	7	2	6	5	3
9	0	5	8	3	6	8	8

Flower: 2

5	3	8	4	2	7	3	9
6	8	5	1	2	2	8	3
2	2	8	7	2	1	5	3
8	6	4	4	2	4	7	10

Flower: 7

10	6	5	10	3	7	8	8
2	2	5	3	2	2	5	2
2	7	7	7	7	2	7	7
3	2	9	4	2	4	7	10

58. Fruit Group

Trace each number. Circle the bowl that has the same number of fruit in it.

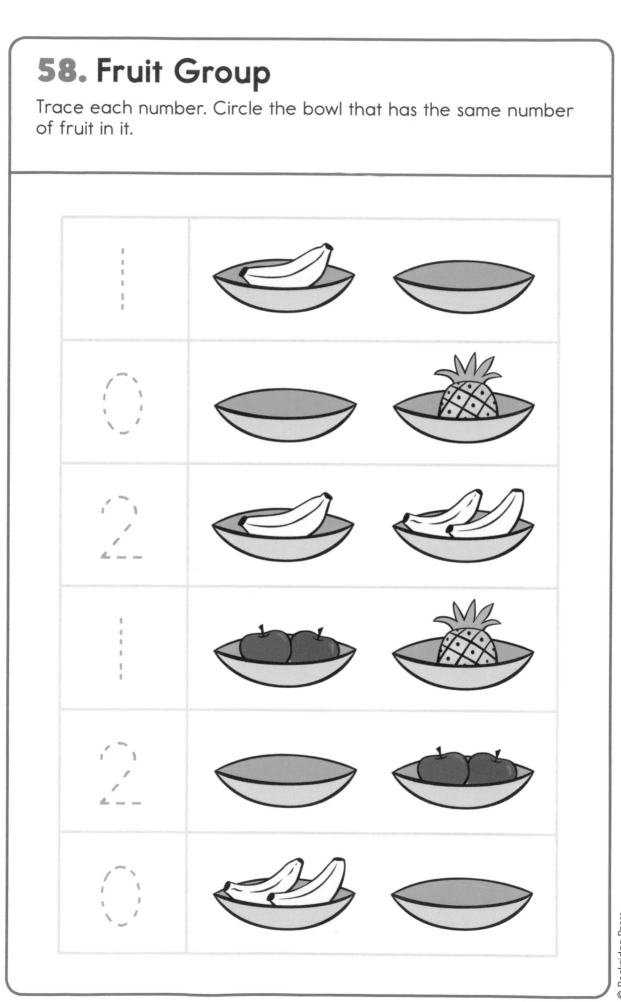

My Kindergarten Workbook

59. In the Jungle

Put an ✗ on 3 . Put a ◯ on 4 🦜.

Put a ▢ on 5 🐸.

60. Roar!

Use the color key to color the picture and see who is the king of beasts.

My Kindergarten Workbook

61. Oliver Follows His Nose

Help Oliver sniff out a way home. Find the path that has dice in order from **1** to **5**. Color the dice as you go.

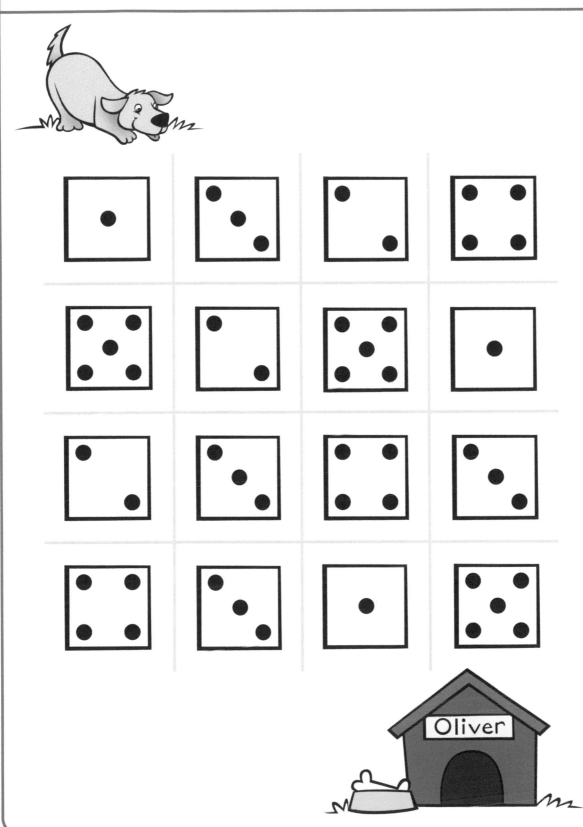

© Rockridge Press

62. More or Less?

In each row, color the group that has more. Put an ✗ on the group that has less.

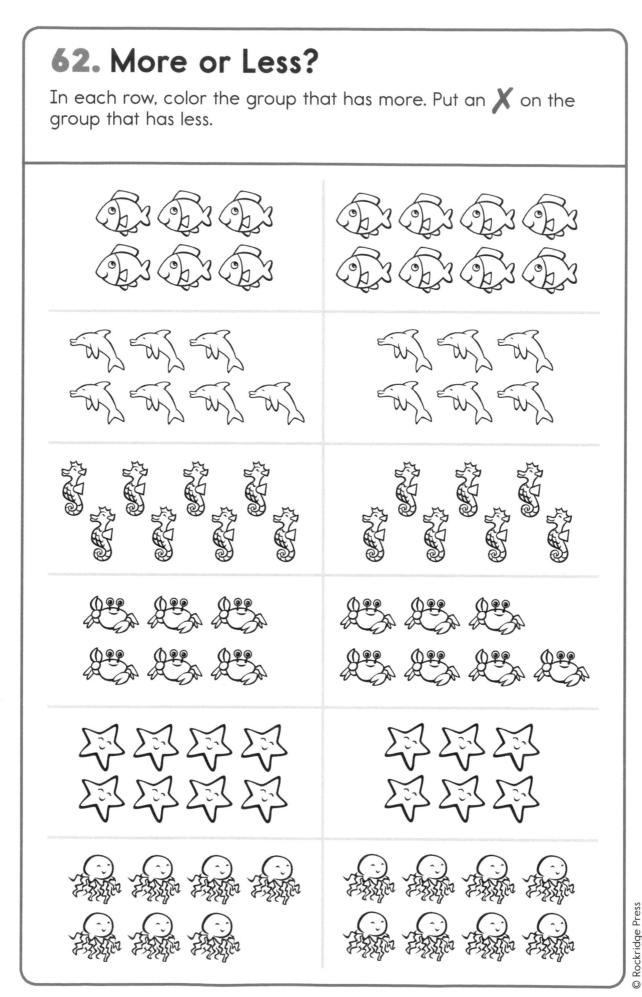

My Kindergarten Workbook

© Rockridge Press

63. Play Ball!

How many times can you find the numbers 6, 7, and 8 hidden in the picture? Write the number in the boxes below.

6: [ ] times   7: [ ] times   8: [ ] times

64. On the Water

Start at the red star. Connect the dots from 1 to 8 to finish the sailboat. Then color the boat so it can sail down the river.

65. How Many More?

The number on each box should match the number of objects inside. Draw in the objects that are missing.

66. Park Pals

How many of each animal do you see in the park? Write the number in the boxes below.

67. A Bear-y Good Reason

Use the code to find out why the teddy bear did not want dessert.

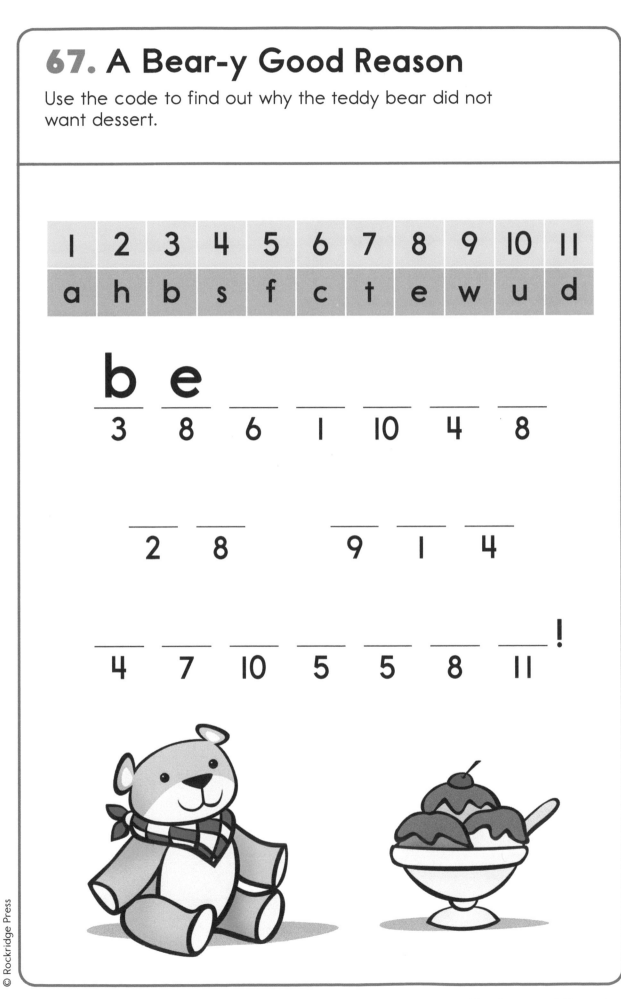

1	2	3	4	5	6	7	8	9	10	11
a	h	b	s	f	c	t	e	w	u	d

b e ___ ___ ___ ___ ___
3 8 6   1   10 4   8

___ ___   ___ ___ ___
 2   8   9   1   4

___ ___ ___ ___ ___ ___ ___!
 4   7   10 5   5   8   11

68. Wonderful Watermelon

Look at the number on each watermelon, and draw that many watermelon seeds.

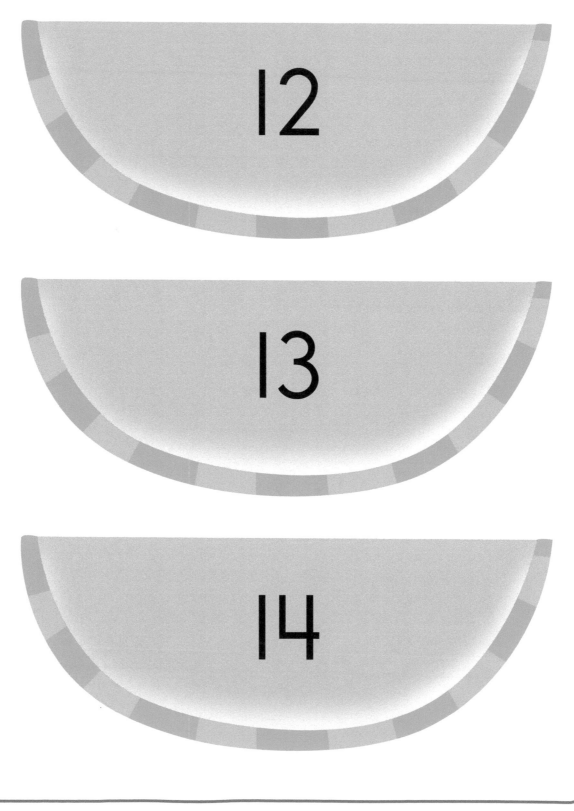

My Kindergarten Workbook

69. Candy Counting

Look at each number on the left, and color in that many candies.

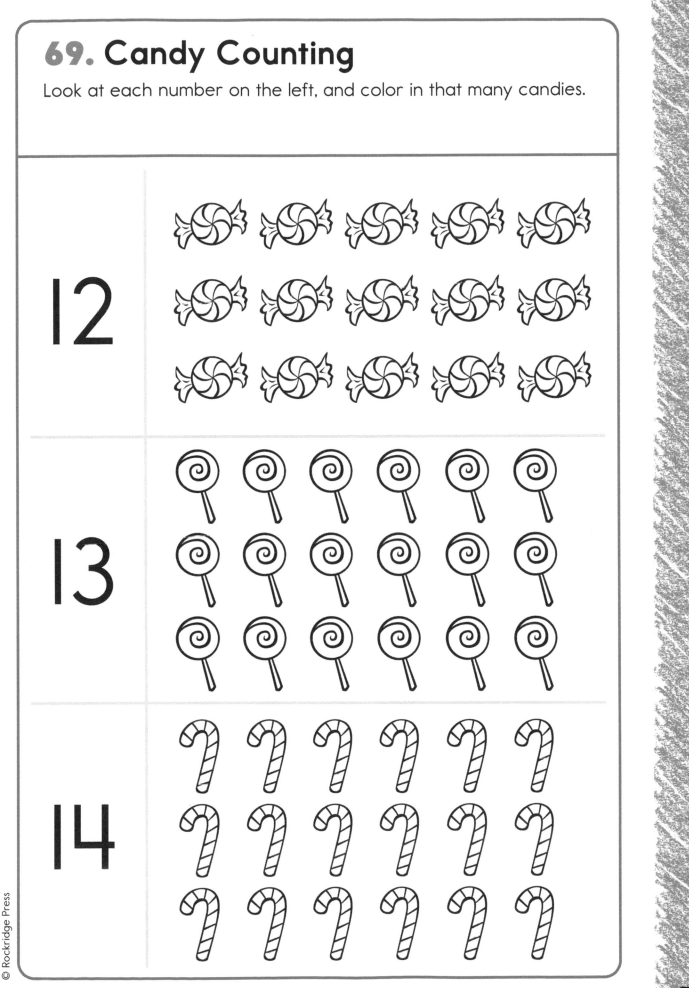

12

13

14

70. Let's Go Swimming!

Follow the numbers from 0 to 14 to help the kids find the pool.

My Kindergarten Workbook

71. Autumn Days

Use the color key to color the picture.

72. More Connect Four

See the number in the flower? Can you find that number repeated 4 times in a row? Draw a line to connect them. Search across, down, or diagonally to solve the puzzle.

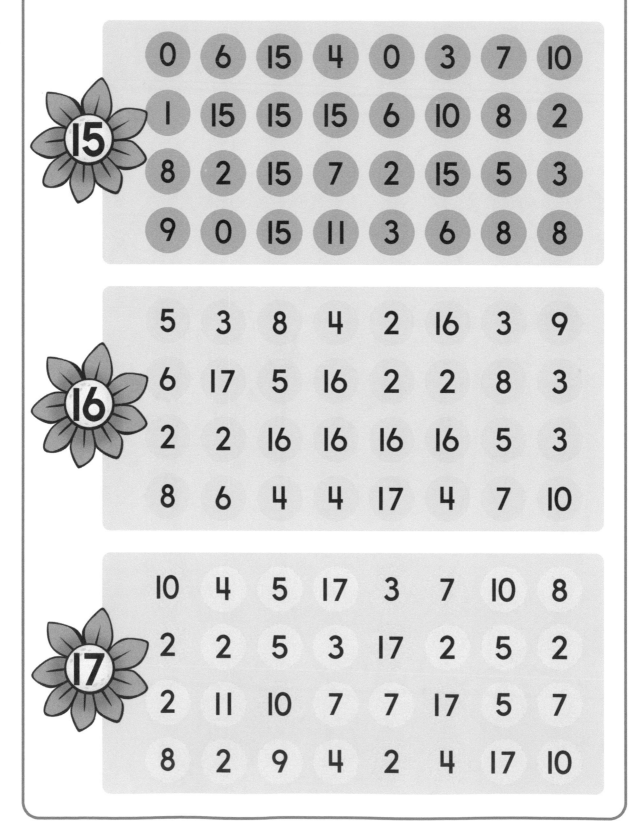

15

0	6	15	4	0	3	7	10
1	15	15	15	6	10	8	2
8	2	15	7	2	15	5	3
9	0	15	11	3	6	8	8

16

5	3	8	4	2	16	3	9
6	17	5	16	2	2	8	3
2	2	16	16	16	16	5	3
8	6	4	4	17	4	7	10

17

10	4	5	17	3	7	10	8
2	2	5	3	17	2	5	2
2	11	10	7	7	17	5	7
8	2	9	4	2	4	17	10

My Kindergarten Workbook

73. On the Prowl

Start at the red star. Connect the dots from 0 to 17 to see who's sneaking through the grass.

74. Yummy Counting

Quick! Before someone eats them, count the number of cookies on each pan and circle the correct number.

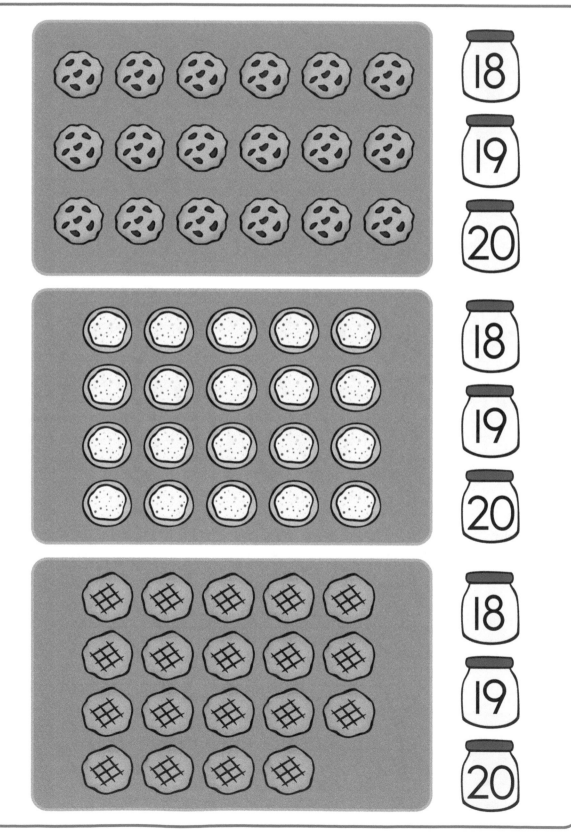

My Kindergarten Workbook

75. Matching Mittens

Draw a line from each mitten to its matching number in the center of the page.

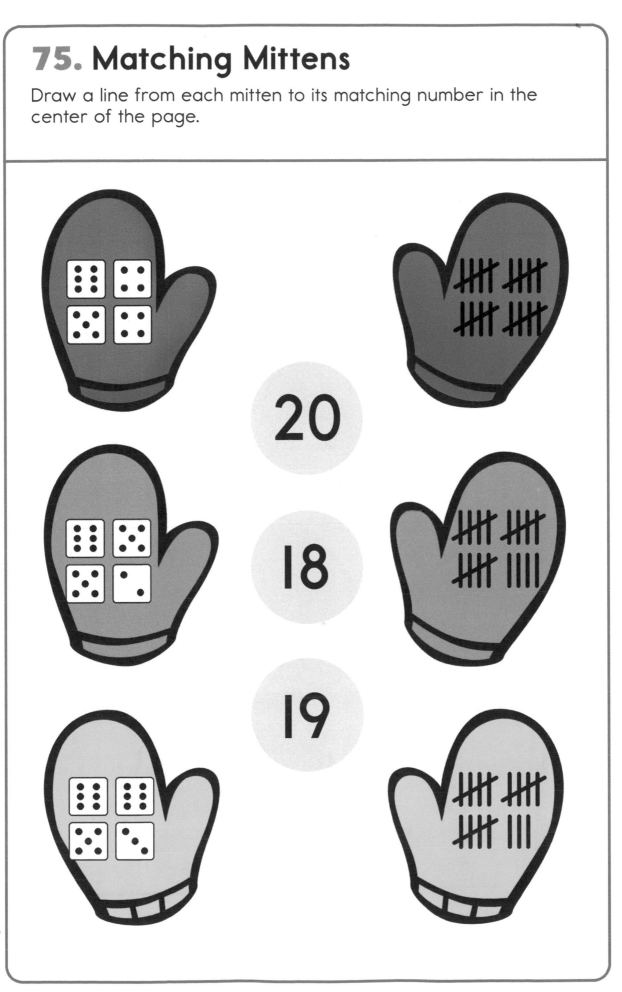

© Rockridge Press

76. At the Beach

Find all of these things you see at the beach. Write how many you found in each box.

lifeguard chair   plastic pails   pairs of sunglasses

book   lounge chairs   bathing suits

umbrellas   towels   seashells

77. A Caterpillar to Count On

Count by 2s out loud. Color those parts on the caterpillar as you go!

78. Who Loves Mud?

Start at the red star. Count by 5s to connect the dots and find out!

79. Down the Rabbit Hole

Help Rachel Rabbit reach her bunnies. Follow the path that counts by 10s.

My Kindergarten Workbook

© Rockridge Press

80. Leaping Lily Pads

Count by 2s, 5s, and 10s to help the frogs hop down the lily pads.

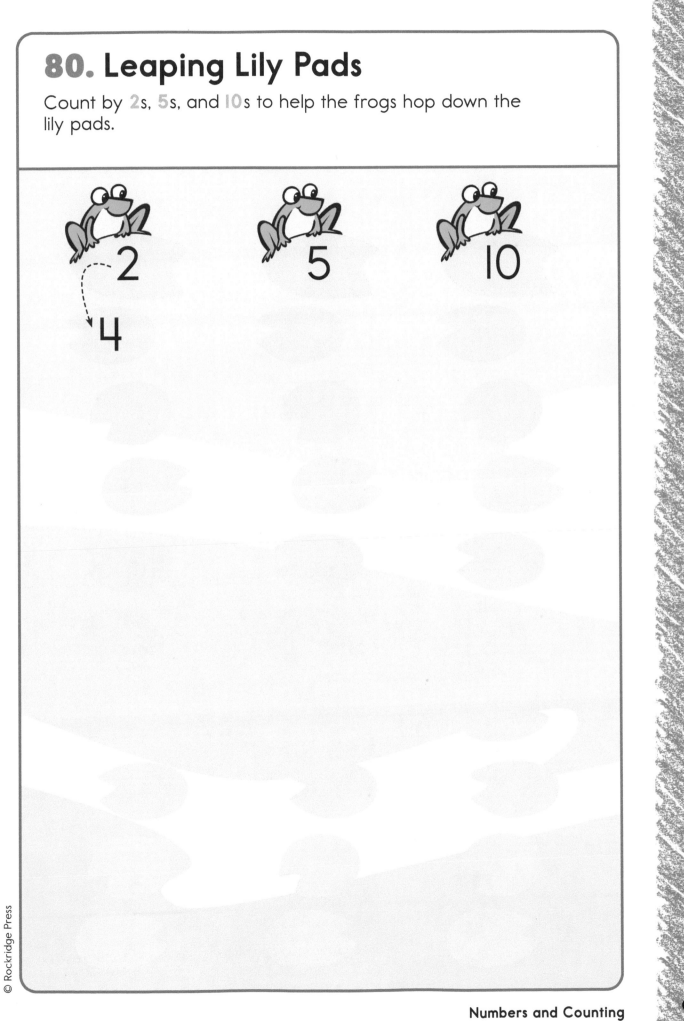

81. It's Raining!

Write in the missing numbers on the raindrops as you count to 100.

		3					8	9	
13		15						20
	24		26			29	
31			35	36				
42					48		50
53		55		58		
62		64		67			
71				76			80
					88	
		95	96			99	

82. The Great Gator Maze

Get Gary back to the gator swamp. Gobble up each number that is greater than the one before to move through the maze.

83. Ladybug Addition

Count the dots on the ladybug's left wing, then add the dots on the right wing to help you solve the problem.

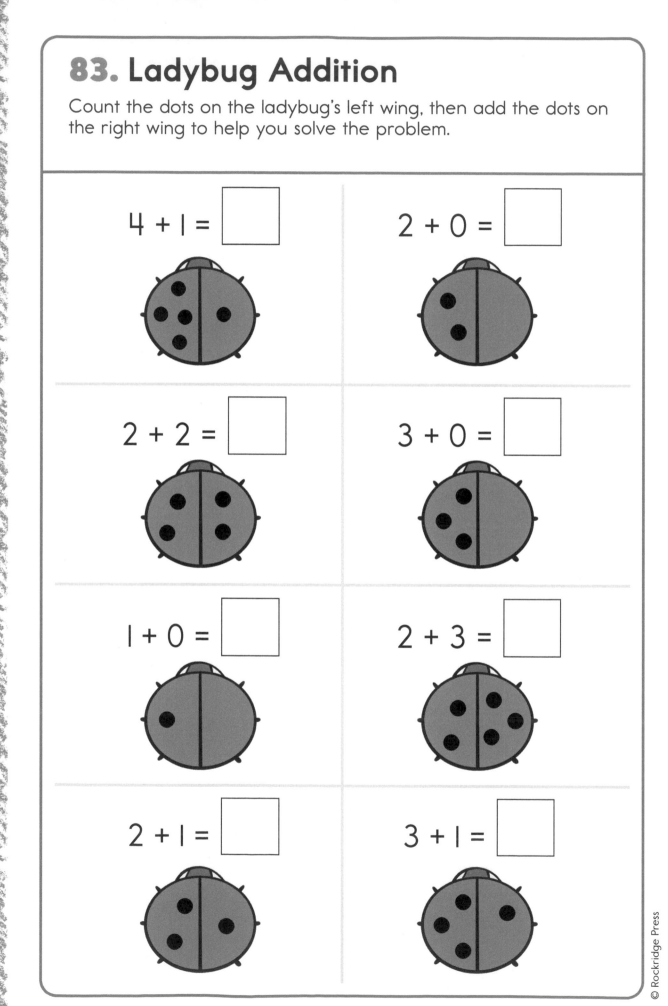

4 + 1 = ☐

2 + 0 = ☐

2 + 2 = ☐

3 + 0 = ☐

1 + 0 = ☐

2 + 3 = ☐

2 + 1 = ☐

3 + 1 = ☐

My Kindergarten Workbook

84. Horsing Around

Help Henry the horse get back home. Solve each addition problem. Then trace the path to the barn.

5+2= ☐   3+0= ☐

6+4= ☐   8+1= ☐   2+2= ☐

4+3= ☐   6+0= ☐   5+3= ☐

4+1= ☐   0+1= ☐

8+2= ☐   3+3= ☐

85. Subtraction Action

Use the pictures to help you solve the problems. Put an ✗ over the number of foods you are subtracting.

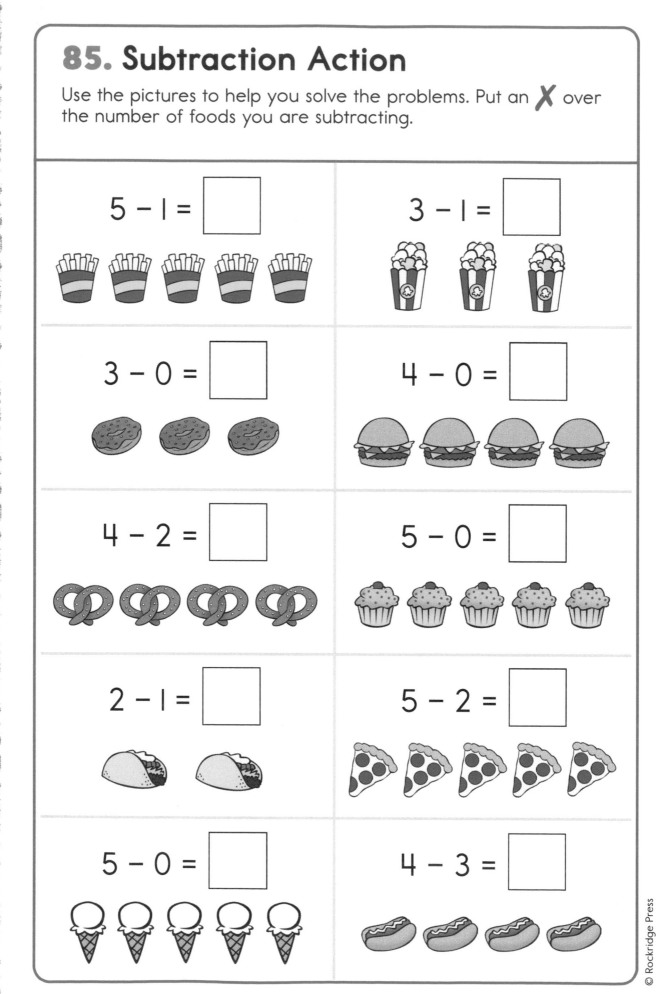

5 − 1 = ☐

3 − 1 = ☐

3 − 0 = ☐

4 − 0 = ☐

4 − 2 = ☐

5 − 0 = ☐

2 − 1 = ☐

5 − 2 = ☐

5 − 0 = ☐

4 − 3 = ☐

My Kindergarten Workbook

86. Subtraction Surprise

Complete the subtraction problems. Then, use the answers and the color key to color the picture.

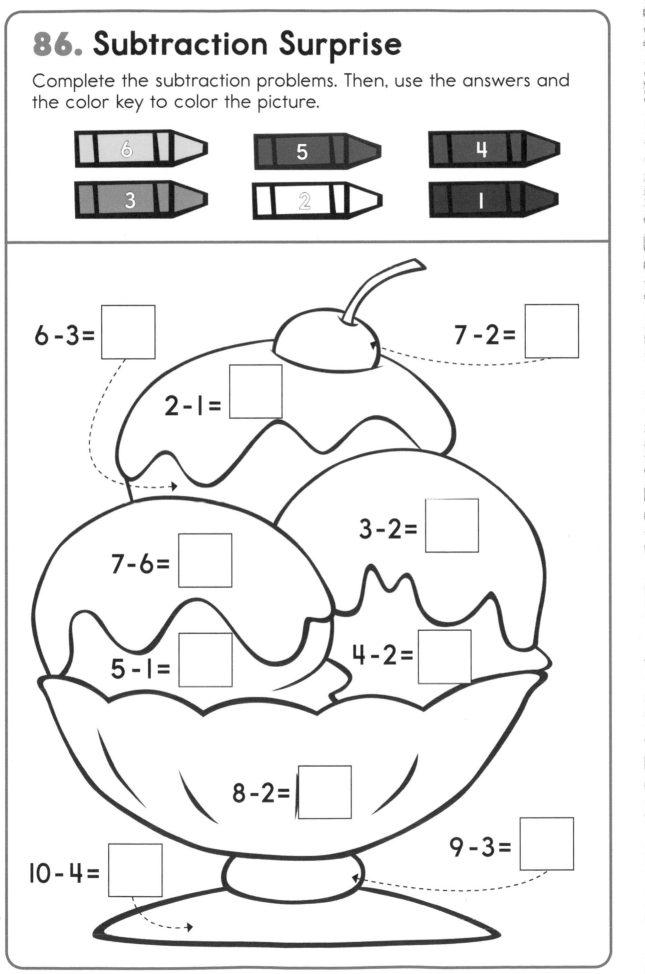

6 - 3 = ☐

7 - 2 = ☐

2 - 1 = ☐

3 - 2 = ☐

7 - 6 = ☐

5 - 1 = ☐

4 - 2 = ☐

8 - 2 = ☐

10 - 4 = ☐

9 - 3 = ☐

© Rockridge Press

87. Cold Cash

First, solve each addition problem. Then, use the letter clues to find out where penguins keep their money.

k	b	w	s	i	n	a	o
3 +2	7 +1	4 +0	2 +1	5 +4	7 +0	1 +5	8 +2

___ ___   ___
 9   7   6

___ ___ ___ ___
 3   7   10   4

___ ___ ___ ___ !
 8   6   7   5

My Kindergarten Workbook

88. Whooo's There?

Find out by solving each subtraction problem. Then, use your answers to connect the dots from 1 to 10.

6 - 2 =

9 - 2 =

8 - 3 =

7 - 1 =

8 - 0 =

7 - 4 =

5 - 3 =

10 - 1 =

6 - 5 =

10 - 0 =

Early Math

89. Our Five Senses

Put a ✔ under all the senses you use with each object.

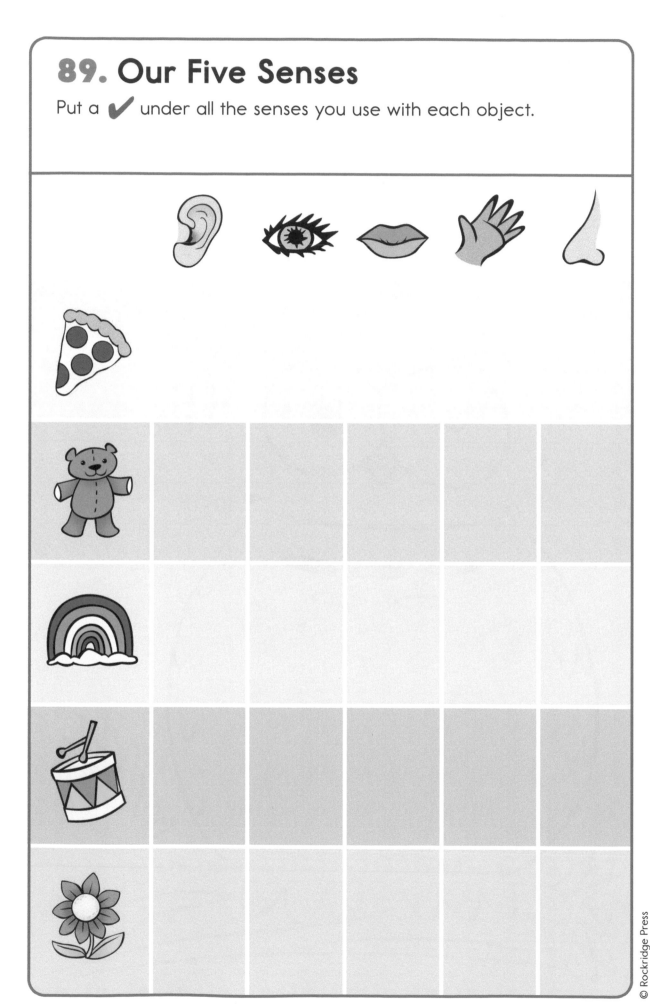

90. A Different Matter

For each row, look at the pictures. Decide if they are a solid, liquid, or gas. Then put an ✗ on the picture that does not belong.

91. Weather Words

Find and circle the words below. Search across, down, and diagonally to solve the puzzle.

sun   cloud   fog   rain   wind   snow

p	r	e	a	u	j	s	c
b	g	a	u	e	s	w	l
w	f	y	i	c	m	u	o
r	o	s	r	n	b	y	u
h	g	a	t	s	u	n	d
w	s	n	s	n	o	w	f
e	w	i	n	d	z	r	g
q	s	w	y	j	e	o	k

My Kindergarten Workbook

92. Season Sorting

Draw a line from each picture to the season in which it belongs.

Winter

Spring

Summer

Fall

93. Is This My Home?

Circle the 3 animals that belong in each habitat. Put an X on the animal that isn't found there.

Arctic

Desert

Ocean

Rain Forest

94. Flowers for Mom

Put these pictures in the right order to make a story. Write 1, 2, 3, 4, 5, or 6 in the boxes to show the correct sequence.

95. How to Build a Snowman

Put these pictures in the right order to make a story. Write 1, 2, 3, 4, 5, or 6 in the boxes to show the correct sequence.

96. Time for School

Help Colton get to school on time. Look at the first clock face. Color the arrow with the matching time, then follow the arrow to the next clock.

97. Community Helpers

Use the picture clues and the word bank to complete the crossword puzzle.

Word Bank

teacher   police officer
doctor   mail carrier
firefighter   farmer

98. What Tools Do I Need?

Draw a line to connect each person in the community to the things they use for their job.

99. Want and Need

Circle the things you need. Put a ✔ on the things you might want.

house

food

phone

clothes

water

pet

shoes

TV

candy

bike

My Kindergarten Workbook

© Rockridge Press

100. Let's Recycle!

It's time to sort the recycling. Color each object the same color as the bin it belongs in.

PAPER · GLASS · ALUMINUM · PLASTIC

101. Our Big World

Find and circle the words below. Search across, down, up, and diagonally to solve the puzzle. Then, fill in the blanks at the bottom of the page to describe where you live.

city state country continent planet

c	b	f	q	u	t	d	o	s	d
o	l	j	a	c	c	v	g	t	z
n	r	z	i	p	i	e	r	a	n
t	o	f	u	x	t	e	b	t	a
i	p	g	v	c	y	y	o	e	t
n	e	l	o	o	c	s	w	b	f
e	x	e	a	b	a	h	o	j	y
n	c	o	u	n	t	r	y	a	r
t	f	g	z	m	e	d	s	n	w
b	u	j	e	o	d	t	y	g	i

I live in the city of _____.

My state is _____.

The country I live in is _____.

It is on the continent called _____.

I live on planet _____.

Answer Key

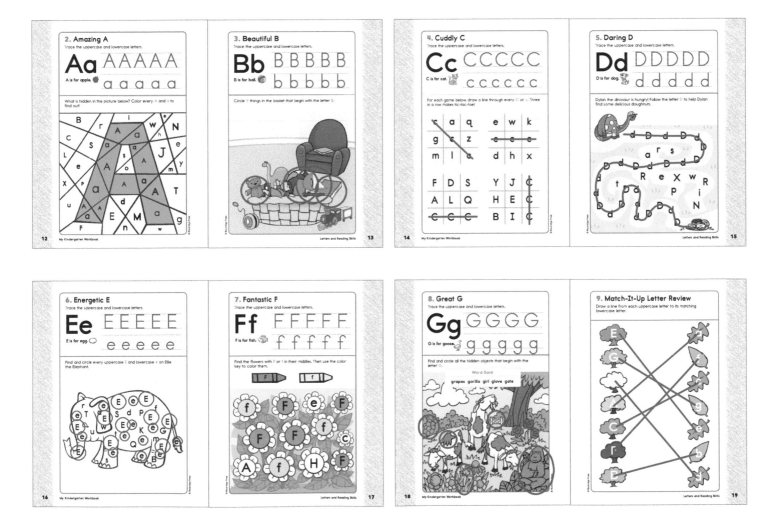

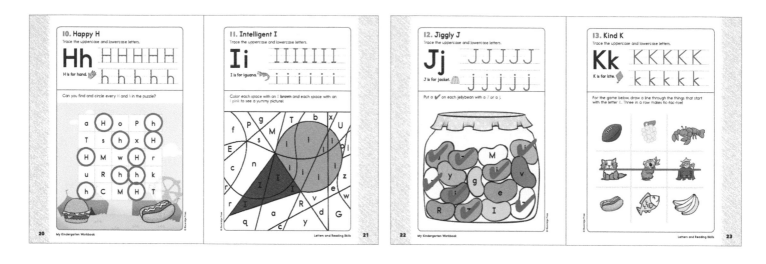

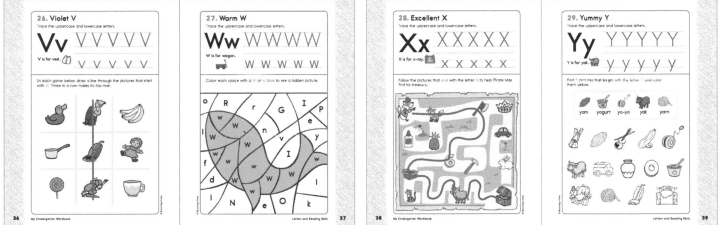

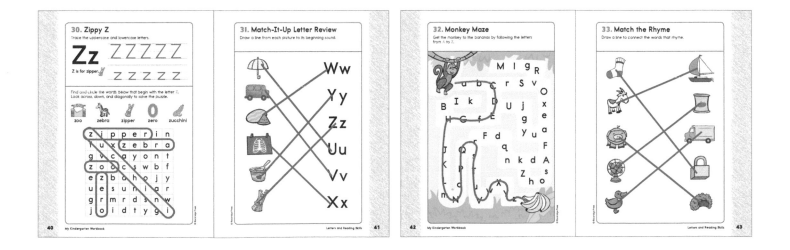

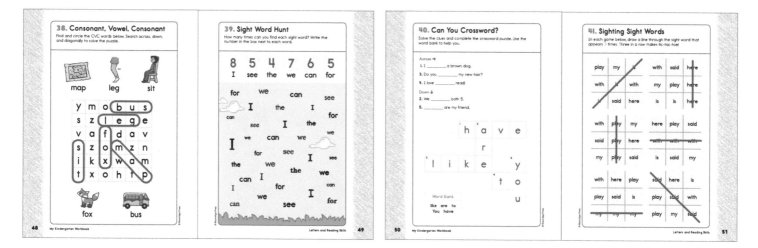

116   Answer Key

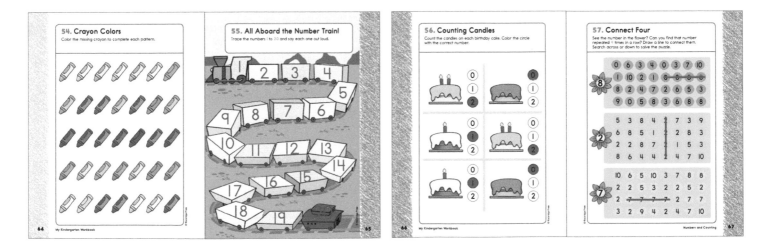

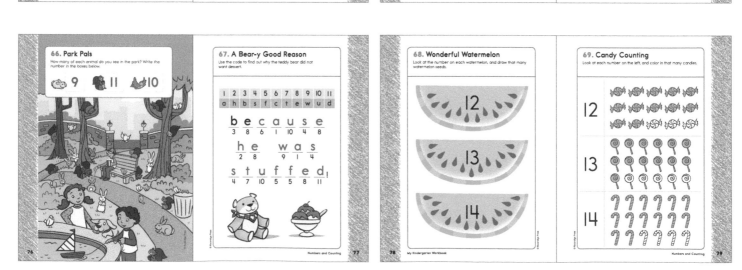

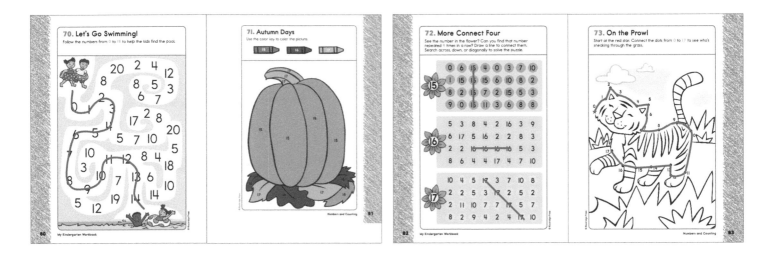

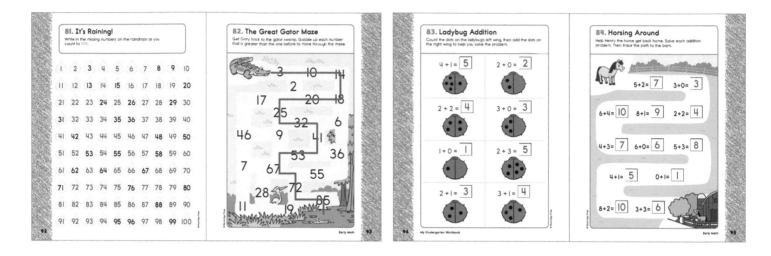

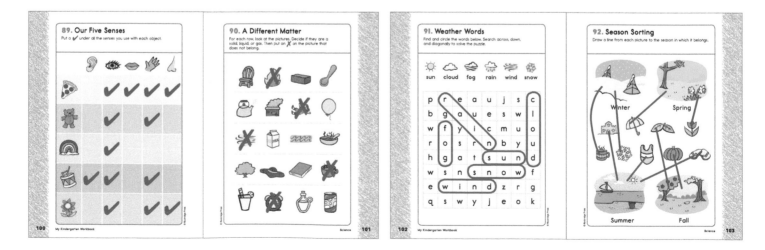

93. Is This My Home?
Circle the 3 animals that belong in each habitat. Put an X on the animal that isn't found there.

Arctic

Desert

Ocean

Rain Forest

104

94. Flowers for Mom
Put these pictures in the right order to make a story. Write 1, 2, 3, 4, 5, or 6 in the boxes to show the correct sequence.

4 | 1
6 | 5
2 | 3

105

95. How to Build a Snowman
Put these pictures in the right order to make a story. Write 1, 2, 3, 4, 5, or 6 in the boxes to show the correct sequence.

5 | 1
3 | 6
4 | 2

106

96. Time for School!
Help Colton get to school on time. Look at the first clock face. Color the arrow with the matching time, then follow the arrow to the next clock.

Social Studies 107

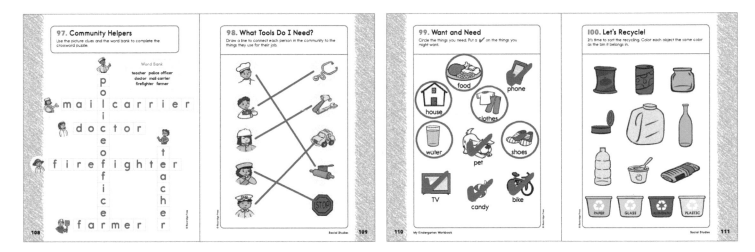

97. Community Helpers
Use the picture clues and the word bank to complete the crossword puzzle.

Word Bank
teacher police officer
doctor mail carrier
firefighter farmer

m a i l c a r r i e r
d o c t o r
f i r e f i g h t e r
f a r m e r

108

98. What Tools Do I Need?
Draw a line to connect each person in the community to the things they use for their job.

STOP

Social Studies 109

99. Want and Need
Circle the things you need. Put a ✓ on the things you might want.

food
phone
house
clothes
water
pet
shoes
TV
candy
bike

110 My Kindergarten Workbook

100. Let's Recycle!
It's time to sort the recycling. Color each object the same color as the bin it belongs in.

PAPER GLASS ALUMINUM PLASTIC

Social Studies 111

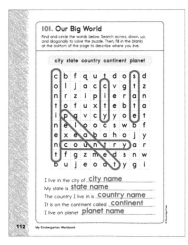

101. Our Big World
Find and circle the words below. Search across, down, up, and diagonally to solve the puzzle. Then, fill in the blanks at the bottom of the page to describe where you live.

city state country continent planet

c b f q u t d o s d
o l j a c c v g t z
n r z i p i e r a n
t o f u x t e b t a
i p a v c y o t e t
n e l o o c s w b f
e x e a b a h o j y
n c o u n t r y a r
t f g z m e d s n w
b u j e o a t y g i

I live in the city of _city name_
My state is _state name_
The country I live in is _country name_
It is on the continent called _continent_
I live on planet _planet name_

112 My Kindergarten Workbook

Answer Key **121**

About the Author

Brittany Lynch holds a bachelor's degree in elementary education and a master's degree in early childhood education. After teaching in the primary grades for eight years, she is now a curriculum author helping provide resources for elementary teachers around the world. Brittany loves to incorporate technology into learning and create hands-on, engaging resources that make learning fun!

Brittany lives in Florida with her husband and dog. In her free time, she enjoys reading, traveling, shopping, and the beach.

To find out more about her work visit TickledPinkInPrimary.com or follow her on Facebook and Instagram: @TickledPinkInPrimary.

You've conquered kindergarten concepts!
You're on top of the world!

_____

has completed all the activities in

My Kindergarten Workbook.

Continue the Learning Fun!

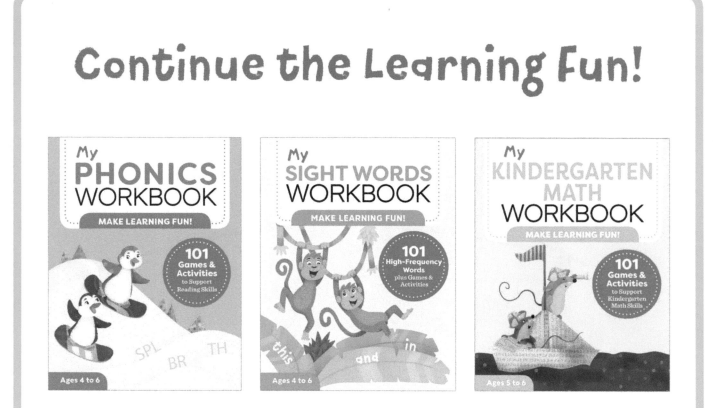

CPSIA information can be obtained
at www.ICGtesting.com
Printed in the USA
JSHW061948220622
27178JS00005B/9